1 MONTH OF
FREE
READING

at

www.ForgottenBooks.com

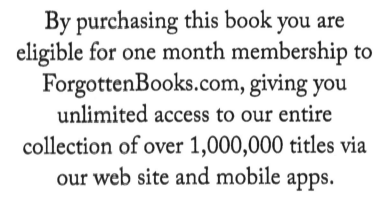

By purchasing this book you are eligible for one month membership to ForgottenBooks.com, giving you unlimited access to our entire collection of over 1,000,000 titles via our web site and mobile apps.

To claim your free month visit:

www.forgottenbooks.com/free1301145

ISBN 978-0-428-65121-3
PIBN 11301145

Uniform Municipal Accounts
Chapter 68, Section 22, 23

Annual Financial Report

OF THE

Town Officers

OF

FRANCONIA, N. H.

INCLUDING THE REPORTS OF THE

Library Trustees and the Trustees
of the Trust Funds

School Board and Superintendent
of the School District

Water Commissioners

FOR THE YEAR ENDING

JANUARY 31, 1940

COURIER PRINTING COMPANY — LITTLETON. N. H.

Town Officers

MODERATOR
Edward J. McKenzie

CLERK
Bertha W. Brooks

SELECTMEN
G. Robert Jesseman   Charles J. Lovett
Alberto L. Nelson

HEALTH OFFICER
Dr. H. L. Johnson

BOARD OF EDUCATION
C. T. Bodwell   Dr. H. L. Johnson   Charlotte Sawyer

WATER COMMISSIONERS
Frank Sanborn   Dr. H. L. Johnson   Victor Clark.

LIBRARY TRUSTEES
Dr. H. L. Johnson
Mrs. Martha Herbert Mrs. C. H. Greenleaf Lucy Priest

HIGHWAY COMMISSIONER
Garold Miller

TREASURER
Edward J. McKenzie

TAX COLLECTOR
Fred H. Jesseman

Town Meeting Warrant
(As known February 15, 1940)

Article 1. To hear reports of committees and agents and act on same and to choose all necessary town officers for the year ensuing.

Article 2. To raise such sums of money as may be necessary to defray town charges for the year ensuing and to appropriate money for the same.

Article 3. To see if the town will vote to raise and appropriate $100.00 for Pine Blister Rust control.

Article 4. To see if the town will vote to authorize the selectmen to provide for the disposal of rubbish and garbage and raise and appropriate money for same and other expenses of the Health Department.

Article 5. To see how much money the town will vote to raise and appropriate for snow removal and maintenance of highways and bridges.

Article 6. To see how much money the town will vote to raise and appropriate for the lighting of streets for the ensuing year.

Article 7. To see how much money the town will vote to raise and appropriate for the general expenses of the highway department.

Article 8. To see how much money the town will vote to raise and appropriate for oiling its roads.

Article 9. To see how much money the town will vote to raise and appropriate for the Abbie Greenleaf Library and salary of its librarian.

Article 10. To see how much money the town will vote to raise and appropriate for the support of the poor.

Article 11. To see how much money the town will vote to raise and appropriate for Old Age Assistance.

Article 12. To see if the town will vote to raise and appropriate the sum of $25.00 for proper observance of Memorial Day.

Article 13. To see if the town will vote to raise and appropriate the sum of $800.00 for parks, playgrounds and recreational development.

Article 14. To see how much money the town will vote to raise and appropriate for care of its cemeteries.

Article. 15. To see if the town will vote to raise and appropriate as follows: $2500.00 to pay the amount maturing on the town building and water works bonds; $1000.00 on outstanding water works purchase notes; and $500.00 on state aid construction note; also the sum of $1800.00 to pay the interest on said indebtedness and on temporary loans.

Article 16. To see if the town will vote to instruct the selectmen to allow a discount for early payment of taxes.

Article 17. To see if the town will vote to allow the selectmen to borrow money in anticipation of taxes.

Article 18. To see if the town will vote to instruct the selectmen to lay out a street connecting Berwick Road and Sunset Lane, and to raise and appropriate money for construction of such portion as the selectmen may deem necessary to meet the public requirements.

Article 19. To see if the town will vote to authorize the selectmen to sell the property located in Easton, N. H., deeded to the town by Lynn L. and Florence Bowles for such price and to such person or persons as in their judgment may seem best.

Article 20. To transact any other business that may legally come before the meeting.

Selectmen's Report

The Board of Selectmen are presenting to the voters of the town a budget for 1940 which has been prepared with the primary thought in mind to reduce the tax rate. If it is accepted by the voters without any changes, and on the basis of the present valuation, there would be a substantial reduction from the 1939 rate of $3.50.

You will note by comparing the estimated expenditures with the appropriations of 1939 that there are several reductions.

Included in the town hall expense is an estimate for painting the building outside and installing an outside entrance to the jail. The community has had considerable free use of the downstairs part of the building and it is the thought of the selectmen that by a pooling of resources and efforts the various organizations could paint the walls and cover the ceiling. A stoker has been installed in the building, the result of which has been a saving in fuel of approximately $150.00.

It was necessary to purchase a road grader this year for which there had been no appropriation, and with which our roads can now be maintained in better condition and at less expense. We do recommend that Dow Avenue Bridge and Church Street Bridge be painted for which an allowance has been made in the budget. Next year the bridges on our Class V roads should be painted.

Most of the T. R. A. money raised last year was spent, as a State requirement, on sections of our Class V roads on which state aid had been received in the past, to bring them up to maintenance. We recommend the raising of our proportion of T. R. A. money this year to be expended on Wallace Hill Road.

The present tool shed is in need of considerable repair and in our opinion it would be advisable to build a new one to properly house tools and machinery, and more conveniently located. We would recommend appropriating $500.00 for the same, which has been included in the budget.

The sum of $152.36 was expended in Elmwood Cemetery in excess of the appropriation. The labor cost is an increasing expense due to the increased amount of mowing. We believe an appropriation of $500.00 will cover the cost of labor for both cemeteries. If the fence in Elmwood Cemetery, damaged by the hurricane, is to be repaired there should be an additional appropriation.

Hereafter any person buying a cemetery lot will be given a deed of same, and any present owner may obtain one.

The Water Commission has met its interest obligations, but has made no payments on the principal. It is the plan of the Commissioners to use such surplus as they may have each year for the gradual improvement of the system rather than to incur further indebtedness at the present time.

The Supervisor of the White Mountain National Forest, the State Forester and the Attorney General have been interviewed in regard to the abatement of the state tax which, until this year, the town has received as a reimbursement for loss of taxes on land taken over by the State and Federal government. The Tobacco Tax Law passed by the last Legislature eliminated the state tax paid by the towns to the state, and since there is now no state tax it was ruled by the Tax Commission that there could not be any abatement.

The matter is now receiving the consideration of the Attorney General and the Tax Commission and we hope to hear from them in the near future. The test case on the constitutionality of the Tobacco Tax Law, we understand, will be tried in the April term of court. If the law is upheld and we get no favorable ruling from the Attorney General, a bill will have to be filed in the forthcoming legislature to provide for a reimbursement to towns having publicly owned lands therein.

G. ROBERT JESSEMAN
CHARLES J. LOVETT
ALBERTO L. NELSON

Selectmen

Inventory of 1939

Land and buildings	$895,775.00
Electric plants	32,500.00
36 horses	3,120.00
2 oxen	150.00
120 cows	6,260.00
21 other neat stock	920.00
4 hogs	40.00
565 fowls	565.00
53 fur-bearing animals	795.00
Wood, lumber, etc.	800.00
Gasoline pumps and tanks	2,390.00
Stock in trade	10,908.00
Mills and machinery	3,850.00
	$958,073.00
Property taxes	$31,882.91
Poll taxes	630.00
Nat'l Bank Stock taxes	35.00
	$32,547.91
Exempted to Soldiers	$4,000.00
Tax rate for Franconia	$3.50

List of Appropriations for 1939

Town officers' salaries	$1,000.00
Town officers' expenses	550.00
Election and registration	25.00
Town hall	1,550.00
Police department	200.00
Fire department	650.00
Blister rust control	100.00
Health department	80.00

Vital statistics	15.00
Town road aid	246.76
Town maintenance	1,200.00
Road oil	300.00
Snow removal	1,000.00
Street lighting	2,000.00
General expenses highway department	1,400.00
Sidewalk construction	200.00
Libraries	375.00
Old Age assistance	300.00
Town poor	1,250.00
Memorial Day	25.00
Parks, playgrounds, rec. development	1,000.00
Cemeteries	500.00
Interest	1,895.00
Payments on principal of debt	5,500.00
School tax	11,600.00
County tax	4,375.34
	$37,337.10

Condensed Budget
Submitted for your consideration for the year 1940

Town officers' salaries	$1,000.00
Town officers' expenses	550.00
Election and registration	85.00
Town hall	1,200.00
Police department	200.00
Fire department	550.00
Blister rust control	100.00
Health department	105.00
Vital statistics	15.00
Town maintenance	1,200.00
Street lighting	2,200.00

Snow removal	1,000.00
General expenses highway department	1,000.00
Road oil	300.00
Town road assistance	245.99
Libraries	375.00
Town poor	1,000.00
Old age assistance	350.00
Memorial Day	25.00
Parks, playgrounds, rec. development	800.00
Cemeteries	500.00
Interest on temporary loans	100.00
Interest on bonds	1,350.00
Interest on long term notes	350.00
Sidewalk construction and repair	150.00
New building	500.00
Payment on bonds	2,500.00
Payment on long term notes	1,500.00
County tax	4,375.34
School district	12,800.00
Legal expense	50.00
	$36,476.33

Schedule of Town Property

Land and buildings	
Town hall and land	$30,000.00
Library, including equipment	28,000.00
Equipment	
Highway department	1,500.00
Fire department	5,000.00
Town office, furniture and fixtures	300.00
Cemetery	100.00
Franconia Water Works	37,000.00
Gravel Pit	200.00
	$102,100.00

Budget of the Town of Franconia

Estimates of Revenue for the Ensuing Year February 1, 1940 to
January 31, 1941 compared with Actual Revenue of the
previous year February 1, 1939 to January 31, 1940

SOURCES OF REVENUE	Actual Revenue Previous Year, 1939	Estimated Revenue Ensuing Year, 1940
From State:		
Interest and Dividends Tax	$ 2,210.02	$ 2,200.00
Gravel	35.80	
T. R. A. refund	160.21	
Savings Bank Tax	356.13	350.00
Refund on knapsack pumps	4.00	
Bounties	5.60	12.40
National Forest Reserve Fund	249.66	125.00
Blister Rust refund	5.80	
From Local Sources Except Taxes:		
Business Licenses and Permits	2.00	
Rent of Town Hall and other buildings	658.00	600.00
Interest received on taxes and deposits	100.29	
Income of Departments:		
(a) Highway, including rental of equipment	76.58	
(b) Fire department	77.50	
Income from Municipally owned Utilities:		
(a) Water departments	1,000.00	1,000.00
Refund to town poor account	180.70	
Motor Vehicle permit fees	860.57	800.00
Dog licenses	87.40	80.00
From Local Taxes other than Property Taxes:		
(a) Poll taxes	570.00	570.00
(b) National Bank Stock Taxes	35.00	35.00
(c) Previous taxes	1,416.36	
(d) Tax sale redemptions	804.95	1,700.00
From Grafton County, relief	395.66	4.00
Sale of Cemetery lots	65.00	
Credit to advertising account	119.72	
Repayment of interest discount	110.00	
Sale of street lamp	3.00	
Donation for Christmas lights	1.00	
Amount Raised by Issue of Bonds or Notes:		
F. W. Horne Co., temporary loans	14,882.12	
F. W. Horne Co., road construction notes	2,397.08	
Bertha Brooks, overpayment		14.71
Cash on hand (surplus)	6,482.28	4,834.15
Total Revenues from all sources except property taxes	$33,352.43	$12,325.26
*Amt. to be raised by property taxes	$33,233.86	$29,958.10
Total revenues	$66,586.29	$42,283.36

Budget of the Town of Franconia

Estimates of Expenditures for the Ensuing Year February 1, 1940 to January 31, 1941 compared with actual expenditures of the previous year February 1, 1939 to January 31, 1940

PURPOSES OF EXPENDITURES	Actual Expend. Previous Year, 1939	Estimated Expend. Ensuing Year, 1940
Current Maintenance Expenses:		
General Government:		
Town Officers' salaries	$ 855.25	$ 1,000.00
Town Officers' expenses	634.40	550.00
Election and registration expenses	26.00	85.00
Expenses Town Hall and other town buildings	1,858.64	1,200.00
Protection of Persons and Property:		
Dog fees	5.20	
Police department	280.86	200.00
Fire department	876.49	550.00
Moth Extermination—Blister Rust	100.00	100.00
Bounties	12.40	
Health:		
Health Department, including hospitals	5.00	5.00
Vital statistics	17.20	15.00
Rubbish and dump	116.09	100.00
Highways and Bridges:		
Town maintenance	1,179.91	1,200.00
Street lighting	2,216.25	2,200.00
General expenses of highway department	1,673.72	1,000.00
Snow removal	1,002.84	1,000.00
Road oil	300.00	300.00
Town road assistance	366.76	245.99
Libraries:		
Libraries	375.00	375.00
Public Welfare:		
Town poor	1,214.03	1,000.00
Old Age assistance	293.25	350.00
County poor	371.66	
Patriotic Purposes:		
Memorial Day and other celebrations	25.00	25.00
Aid to soldiers and their families	116.54	
Recreation:		
Parks and playgrounds, including advertising	996.40	800.00
Public Service Enterprises:		
Cemeteries	662.98	500.00
Interest:		
On temporary loans	135.12	100.00
On bonded debt	1,385.00	1,350.00

On long term notes	410.00	350.00
Overpayment to town clerk	14.71	

Outlay for New Construction and Permanent Improvement:

Sidewalk construction and repair	334.23	150.00
New lands and buildings		500.00
New equipment	414.53	
Moving shovel	66.20	
Land damage	4.00	

Payment on Principal of Debt:

(a) Bonds	2,500.00	2,500.00
(b) Long term notes	2,000.00	1,500.00
(c) Temporary loans	19,000.00	

Payments to Other Governmental Divisions:

County taxes	4,375.34	4,375.34
Legal expenses	50.91	50.00
Payments to School districts	12,751.20	18,607.03
Refunds	89.84	
Taxes bought by town	2,639.19	
Total Expenditures	$61,752.14	$42,283.36

Comparative Statement of Appropriations and Expenditures Fiscal Year Ending January 31, 1940

	Appro.	Expenditures	Balance	Overdraft
Town officers' salaries	$1,000.00	$ 855.25	$ 144.75	
Twn ... xpns	550.00	634.40		84.40
... nd registration	25.00	26.00		1.00
Twn hall	1,550.00	1,200.64*	349.36	
Police department	200.00	280.86		80.86
Fire ... pmnt	650.00	79*		144.49
Blister ... control	100.00	1.9*	5.80	
Health department	80.00	121.09		41.09
Vital ...	15.00	7.20		2.20
Twn ...d aid	246.76	206.55*	40.21	
Twn maintenance	1,200.00	1,155.50*	44.50	
Road oil	300.00	300.00		
Snow removal	1,000.00	1,002.84		2.84
Street lighting	2,000.00	2,216.25		216.25
General ... highway	40.00	1,673.72		273.72
Sidewalk construction and repair	200.00	334.23		134.23
Libraries	375.00	375.00		
Old Age ...	300.00	293.25	6.75	
Town poor	1,250.00	1,033.33*	216.67	
Memorial Day	25.00	25.00		
Parks, playgrounds, etc	1,...00	876. 8*	123.32	
New rnt	500.00	662.98		162.98
		414.53		414.53
Interest	1895.00	1,820.12*	74.88	
Payments on principal of debt	5,500.00	4,500.00	1,000.00	
School ...	11,600.00	6,000.00	balance due school	
... ty tax	4,375.34	4,375.34		

Net Balance $447.65

*These figures show net expenditures. The credit to each one has been deducted so that a true figure is given in the balance or overdraft column.

Treasurer's Report

Cash on hand, February 1, 1939	$6,482.28
Received from Tax Collector	36,160.46
Received from State of N. H.:	
Hedgehog bounties	5.60
Sale of gravel	35.80
Refund on knapsack pumps	4.00
Refund to T. R. A.	160.21
Savings Bank tax	356.13
Interest and dividends tax	2,210.02
Blister rust refund	5.80
National Forest reserve fund	249.66
Grafton county, relief	395.66
Town Clerks, auto permits	860.57
Town Clerks, dog licenses	87.40
Water department, interest	1,000.00
Milk license	2.00
Rent of town hall	658.00
Sale of cemetery lots	65.00
Temporary loans	14,882.12
Work on private roads	19.71
Work on cemetery roads	4.70
James J. Viette, gravel	13.25
Charles Flanagan, tile	6.70
Paul Stevens, scrap iron	1.50
James Wafer, tar and sand	30.72
Sale of advertising	103.00
Greenleaf Civics club, ½ cost of sign	16.72
Butter Hill road notes	2,397.08
Repayment of interest discount	110.00
Christmas lights donation	1.00
Sale of street lamp	3.00

| Town of Lisbon for fires | 77.50 | |
| Refund to town poor | 180.70 | $66,586.29 |

| Total payments as per Selectmen's orders | $61,752.14 |

| Cash on hand February 1, 1940 | $4,834.15 |

Tax Collector's Report

Tax levy 1939 committed to Collector
Property tax	$33,392.56	
Poll tax	630.00	
National Bank Stock tax	35.00	
Additions Property tax	133.00	
Additions Poll tax	22.00	$34,212.56

1938 taxes uncollected Feb 1, 1939	1,420.85	
1937 taxes uncollected Feb. 1, 1939	12.62	
1936 taxes uncollected Feb. 1, 1939	37.97	$1,471.44

| Tax sale redemptions | 804.95 |
| Interest collected | 100.29 |

| | $36,589.24 |

Treasurer's receipts to collector	$36,160.46	
1939 abatements	230.18	
1938 abatements	12.00	
1939 taxes uncollected Feb. 1, 1940	133.52	
1938 taxes uncollected Feb. 1, 1940	36.21	
1937 taxes uncollected Feb. 1, 1940	12.62	
1936 taxes uncollected Feb. 1, 1940	4.25	$36,589.24

Additions property tax:
| McKenzie, Inc. | $105.00 |

Etta M. Howard	28.00	133.00

Additions poll tax:

Horace Nelson	2.00
Dorothy Nault	2.00
Rupert Carpenter	2.00
Alice Bewley	2.00
Fletcher Brown	2.00
Richard Bowles	2.00
Merle Sherman (1938)	2.00
Clarence Brungot (1938)	2.00
John Lovett (1938)	2.00
Charles Chase (1938)	2.00
Horace Nelson (1938)	2.00

22.00

Tax levy 1938 collected:

Ruth Carpenter	3.00	
Mrs. Mabel Carpenter	2.00	
Henry A. Cook	37.80	
Harry S. Davis	41.66	
Roger Enderson	2.00	
Elizabeth Later, Est.	40.68	
Murdock Peabody	2.00	
James T. Wafer	50.00	
Nat'l. F. Perkins, Est.	1,186.50	
George Delage	5.00	
Mrs. Warren Miller	2.00	1,372.64

Tax levy 1936 collected:

Blanche Peabody	33.72

Tax sale redemptions:

Harry S. Davis, 1938	192.64
Ernest E. Herbert, 1938	40.00
Frank Hawes, 1938	29.10
Warren Miller, 1938	22.50

Hubert F. Krantz, 1938		
(abated $12.83)	474.60	
Elizabeth Later, Est., 1938	46.11	804.95

Abatements of 1939:

Quentin Aulis	2.00	
Hazel H. Bean	17.50	
Laura S. Corey	5.25	
Mrs. Fred DeWitt	2.00	
Marion Dexter	2.00	
Mrs. Robert Gardner	2.00	
Charles E. Harriman	2.00	
Elroy Harriman, Sr.	2.00	
Elizabeth Horton	28.00	
Harry Simpson	2.00	
Mrs. Harry Simpson	2.00	
Gladys Taylor	2.00	
Meda B. Wood	2.00	
Nellie Farrington, error	140.00	
Walter Hendricks	17.50	
Max Schoelhoffer	1.93	230.18

Abatements of 1938:

Mrs. Ruth Bond	2.00	
Mrs. Roger Enderson	2.00	
Albert Marcou	2.00	
Mrs. Albert Marcou	2.00	
George Mitton	2.00	
Mrs. George Mitton	2.00	12.00

Tax levy 1939 uncollected:

Elsie Aldrich	2.00
Harry Bellan	2.00
Mrs. Harry Bellan	2.00
Robert Bean	2.00

L. L. Bowles	2.00	
Mariette Bowles	2.00	
Bertha Brooks	12.80	
L. C. Brooks	2.00	
Florence Carpenter	2.00	
Mabel Carpenter	2.00	
Geo. P. Cotnoir	2.00	
Albert Delage	2.10	
Annie Delage	2.00	
George Delage	17.50	
Rena Harlow	2.00	
Lurline Hawes	2.00	
Elizabeth Harriman	2.00	
Elroy Harriman, Jr.	2.00	
Margaret Harriman	2.00	
Bertram Herbert	2.00	
Eliza Herbert	25.00	
Wm. Hopkins	2.00	
Edward Houghton	2.00	
Mrs. Moody Huntoon	2.00	
Mrs. Chas. Kosch	2.00	
Geo. and Janette Manley	15.00	
George Manley	2.00	
Janette Manley	2.00	
Wm. Mayhew	3.00	
Bruce Parfremont	2.00	
Edw. B. Parker	2.00	
May E. Pelletier	2.00	
Max Schoelhoffer	6.12	133.52

Tax levy 1938 uncollected:

Elsie Aldrich	2.00
Mrs. Frank Hawes	2.00
Mrs. Charles Kosch	2.00
Joe Kosch	2.00
Howard Miller	5.09

Mrs. Archie Pelletier	2.00	
George E. Dexter	3.39	
George Delage	15.34	
Ruth Carpenter	2.39	36.21

Tax levy 1937 uncollected:

Perley Goodwin	10.62	
Edward Houghton	2.00	12.62

Tax levy 1936 uncollected:

Warren Miller	4.25

Tax Sales to Town of Franconia unredeemed:

1939	Nat'l F. Perkins Est.		
	(April sale)	1,230.41	
	Ruth Carpenter	16.00	
	Frank Hawes	32.00	
	Guy Harriman	23.11	
	Ernest Herbert	62.22	
	Warren Miller	23.11	
	J. P. Collins & H. P. Cross	67.31	
	George Dexter	5.11	
	Forest Products Co.	17.53	
	Mrs. E. Huntington	38.86	
	Nat'l. F. Perkins Estate	999.64	
	Elizabeth Later Estate	45.97	
	Charles Kosch	31.81	2,593.08
1938	Frank Casey	83.53	
	Ernest E. Herbert, balance	27.29	
	Forest Products Co.	17.07	
	Amelia J. Persons	49.12	177.01
1937	Hubert F. Krantz	531.54	
	D. M. Persons	5.81	
	Amelia Persons	37.04	574.39
1936	D. M. Persons	6.76	
	Amelia Persons	44.01	50.77

Town of Franconia   **Balance**

ASSETS

Cash in hands of Treasurer	$4,834.15	
Accounts receivable:		
State of N. H. bounties	12.40	
Bertha Brooks, overpayment	14.71	
Grafton County, January relief	4.00	
Due from tax sales	3,395.25	
Uncollected taxes	186.60	
Total Assets		$8,447.11
Excess of liabilities over assets (net debt)		54,859.92

$63,307.03

LIABILITIES

Due School District:

Balance of appropriation	5,600.00	
Dog licenses less fees	82.20	
One-half 1939 N. F. R. F.	124.83	

Total current liabilities	$5,807.03
Balance of Water Works purchase notes, payable $1,000 each year at the Littleton National Bank with interest at 3%, due in January of each year	$10,000.00
State Aid Construction notes, payable $500.00 in March 1940, $1,000.00 in March 1941, $1000.00 in March 1942, interest at 2%	2,500.00
Town building and water works construction 3% bonds, due $2,500.00 in September of each year, 1940 to 1957 inclusive	45,000.00

Total outstanding bonds and long term notes	$57,500.00

Total liabilities	$63,307.03

DETAILED STATEMENT OF RECEIPTS

From local and National Bank
  Stock taxes:
  1939 property taxes inc. Nat'l
    bank stock $33,268.86
  1939 poll taxes   570.00
  Previous property and
    poll taxes   1,416.36
  Tax sales redemptions   804.95
  Interest   100.29 $36,160.46

From State of New Hampshire:
  Hedgehog bounties   5.60
  Sale of gravel   35.80
  Refund on knapsack pumps   4.00
  Refund to T. R. A.   160.21
  Savings Bank tax   356.13
  Interest and dividends tax   2,210.02
  Blister Rust refund   5.80
  Nat'l. Forest Reserve fund   249.66   3,027.22

From Grafton County·
  Relief reimbursement   395.66
From Town Clerks:
  Auto permits   860.57
  Dog licenses   87.40   947.97

From Water department, a/c interest   1,000.00
Business licenses and permits, milk license   2.00
Rent of town hall:
  Post Office   450.00

(CONTINUED ON PAGE 26)

Payments· For the·year ending Jan. 31, 1940

SUMMARY OF PAYMENTS

General Government:
Town officers' salaries	$855.25	
Town officers' expenses	634.40	
Election and registration	26.00	
Town hall·expenses	1,858.64	$3,374.29

Protection of Persons and Property:
Police department	280.86	
Fire department	876.49	
Blister rust	100.00	
Bounties	12.40	
Damage by dogs and fees	5.20	1,274.95

Health:
Health department	5.00	
Vital statistics	17.20	
Rubbish and dump	116.09	138.29

Highways and Bridges:
Town Maintenance	1,179.91	
Snow removal	1,002.84	
Road oil	300.00	
Town road assistance	366.76	
Street lighting	2,216.25	
General expense Highway department	1,673.72	6,739.48

Libraries		375.00
Public Welfare:		
Old Age assistance	293.25	

(CONTINUED ON PAGE 27)

Lafayette Grange	78.50	
Saint Mary's in the Mountains	12.50	
Franconia Ski club	40.00	
White Mountain Garden Club	25.00	
Yale Puppeteers	25.00	
Greenleaf Civics Club	16.00	
Women's Union	1.00	
Cash	10.00	658.00

Sale of Cemetery lots:

Elizabeth Gilman	25.00	
Lawrence Gilman	25.00	
Harry Benedict	15.00	65.00

Temporary loans:

F. W. Horne Co.	15,000.00	
Less interest discount	117.88	14,882.12

Road repairs:

Armitt Brown	13.62	
W. B. Symmes, Jr.	3.48	
Forest Hills Hotel Co.	2.61	19.71

Other Highway department income:

Trustees of Trust Funds, hauling loam	$ 4.70	
James J. Viette, sale of gravel	13.25	
Charles Flanagan, tile	6.70	
Paul Stevens, scrap iron	1.50	
James Wafer, tar and sanding	30.72	$56.87

(CONTINUED ON PAGE 28)

Payments (Continued)

Town poor	1,214.03	
County poor	371.66	
Soldier's aid	116.54	1,995.48
Patriotic Purposes:		
Memorial Day	25.00	
Advertising	834.51	
Parks and playgrounds	46.89	
Special summer patrol	115.00	1,021.40
Cemeteries		662.98
Unclassified:		
Legal expenses	50.91	
Taxes bought by Town	2,639.19	
State of N. H., move shovel	66.20	
F. H. Jesseman, 1938 refund	37.00	
Norman Fox, Lisbon Town clerk	26.31	
Land damages	4.00	
Hazel Bean, tax refund	26.53	
Bertha Brooks, overpayment	14.71	2,864.85
Interest		1,930.12
New Construction and Improvements:		
Sidewalk construction and repair	334.23	
New equipment	414.53	748.76
Indebtedness payments:		
Temporary loans	19,000.00	
Bonds and long term notes	4,500.00	23,500.00
Payments to other Governmental Divisions:		
County tax	4,375.34	

(CONTINUED ON PAGE 29)

Credit to Recreation account:
  Sale of advertising,
    directory sign $103.00
  Greenleaf Civics Club,
    ½ cost small sign   16.72 $119.72

Butter Hill Road notes:
  F. W. Horne Co. $2,397.08
F. W. Horne Co., repayment on
  interest discount $110.00
Greenleaf Civics Club, Christmas lights   1.00
Sale of street lamp   3.00
Fire Department, Town of Lisbon   77.50
Refund to Town Poor:
  Case No. 1 $12.65
  Case No. 2   3.00
  Warren Miller for George Miller   5.00
  Wallace Miller for rent   10.00
  Transient   .05
  Joseph Deatte, L. L. Bowles camp   150.00 $180.70

Total receipts $60,104.01
Feb. 1, 1939 cash on hand   6,482.28

                                                 $66,586.29

Payments (Continued)

School district	12,751.20	17,126.54
Total payments		$61,752.14
Feb. 1, 1940 Cash on hand		4,834.15

$66,586.29

Town Clerks' Reports

Automobile permits	$254.65
Dog licenses	4.00

Remittances to Treasurer	$258.65

HOLLIS H. WHITCOMB,
Town Clerk

Automobile permits	$605.92
Dog licenses	83.40

Remittances to Treasurer	$689.32

BERTHA W. BROOKS,
Town Clerk

Detail 1—Town Officers' Salaries

G. Robert Jesseman, selectman	$ 166.90
Charles J. Lovett, selectman	98.00
A. L. Nelson, selectman	80.10
Hollis Whitcomb, town clerk	12.00
Hollis Whitcomb, auto permits	14.50
William P. Hodge, selectman	12.00
Bertha Brooks, town clerk	100.00
Bertha Brooks, auto permits	45.25
Bertha Brooks, general records	29.05
Edward J. McKenzie, treasurer	30.00
Fred H. Jesseman, tax collector	150.00
Louise Vintinner, auditor	20.00
Bertram L. Herbert, overseer of poor	23.80
L. H. Vintinner, overseer of poor	73.65
	$855.25

Detail 2—Town Officers' Expenses:

William P. Hodge, selectman	$ 2.40
A. L. Nelson, selectman	.50
G. Robert Jesseman, selectman	12.20
C. J. Lovett, selectman	11.35
F. H. Jesseman, tax collector	10.50
Bertha Brooks, town clerk	10.35
L. H. Vintinner, overseer of poor	21.38
Hollis Whitcomb, town clerk	.70
Bertram L. Herbert, overseer of poor	6.50
Eva B. Hodge, making taxes	17.00
Theda Shores, clerical	2.30
L. H. Vintinner, town reports, clerical	121.18
Willis Herbert, postage	30.06
Franconia Insurance Agency, bonds	51.00

Crowley & Lunt, directory	10.00
Tribune Publishing Co., tax bills	.2.10
White Mountain Studio, freshet pictures	4.75
Edson C. Eastman, supplies	46.39
Courier Printing Co., town reports, supplies	202.09
Northern Office Supply adding machine	2.00
New England Tel. and Tel. Co.	38.90
Associ. N. H. Assessors, dues	2.00
Wheeler & Clark, equipment and supplies	28.75
	$634.40

Detail 3—Election and Registration:

Harold Bowles, supervisor	$ 7.00
Roy Bowles, supervisor	7.00
Paul H. Rich, supervisor	7.00
E. J. McKenzie, moderator	5.00
	$26.00

Detail 4—Town Hall Expenses:

George Miller, janitor	$120.41
Raymond Miller, janitor	51.25
Pliny Goodwin, janitor and policing	207.80
George Miller, janitor supplies	1.20
R. E. Peabody, Inc., janitor supplies	3.73
F. E. Aldrich & Son, supplies and wood	7.05
Littleton Hardware Co., Inc., equipment and supplies	17.36
Young Bros. Co., stepladder	7.80
Nancy M. Daniels, repair flag	1.00
Ray's Home Service, supplies	5.00
J. I. Holcomb Mfg. Co., floor varnish and supplies	16.27
A. L. Nelson, sand urns	3.60
Cooney Furniture Co., piano lamp	1.35
Parker Drug Stores, Inc., floor wax	2.36

Alison Peters, paint flagpole	5.00
Northern Coal Co., coal	193.53
W. F. Parker & Son, coal	93.00
Public Service Co. of N. H., lights	108.96
Water rent	24.25
C. M. Vintinner, janitor supplies	2.54
I. F. Pennock & Son, shelf lumber	5.46
Elmer Blodgett, building shelves	2.30
A. G. Cyr, stoker	515.00
Rhett R. Scruggs, repairs to boiler	7.00
Franconia Insurance Agency, building and boiler insurance	307.52
Wayside Gardens, lawn seed, etc.	6.50
Silas Taylor, cutting hay	5.00
Waldo Nelson, labor on tank	62.07
Garold Miller, haul coal and gravel	14.31
A. E. Morse, plumbing	25.23
Florence Bowles, labor	4.20
Elsie Aldrich, labor	1.90
Perley Goodwin, labor	1.60
M. P. Gallagher, tune piano	5.00
O. N. Aldrich, labor	2.80
Donald Taylor, labor	9.80
G. R. Jesseman, express	1.00
Lewis Express, express	1.25
Houle's Electric Shop, electric repairs	5.84
Quentin Aulis, labor	1.40
	$1,858.64

(Credit to this account of $658.00)
Detail 5—Police Department:

Bertram Herbert, salary	$ 73.00
Bertram Herbert, expense	10.40
George Miller, salary	3.50
Winton Hunt, salary	3.15

Merton Shores, salary	14.50
C. M. Vintinner, salary	106.15
C. M. Vintinner, expense	35.60
Bellows & Baldwin, caps	7.50
C. M. Vintinner, badge	2.21
W. S. Darley Co., badge	2.00
Spencer Drug Co., equipment	22.85
	$280.86

Detail 6—Fire Department:

Paul H. Rich, chief's salary	75.00
P. J. Ball, assistant chief's salary	25.00
P. J. Ball, salary of 19 firemen	309.50
Central Garage, fire truck expense	19.28
Littleton Village District, Academy and Casey fire	114.00
P. J. Ball, burning Corey and McGuire fields (48 men)	38.75
H. S. Davis, Crocker Woods and Scragg Hill fires, for firemen	78.90
John H. Foster, knapsack pumps	25.00
J. J. Coney, express on pumps	1.92
James W. Smith, water cans	30.00
Paul Welch, labor water holes	11.55
Ernest Herbert, labor water holes	14.80
O. N. Aldrich, labor water holes	12.80
Garold Miller, labor water holes	2.70
Donald Taylor, labor water holes	2.00
Elroy Harriman, labor water holes	16.00
Roscoe Bean, labor water holes	16.00
E. J. McKenzie, lumber	12.64
Franconia Insurance Agency, pumper insurance	70.65
	$876.49

(Refund on knapsack pumps $4.00)
(Town of Lisbon, fires $77.50)

Detail 7—White Pine Blister Rust	$100.00

(Refund from State of N. H. $5.80)

Detail 8—Bounties:

Albert Judd, 18 hedgehogs	$ 3.60
Wilfred Wessels, 21 hedgehogs	4.20
Vernon Smith, 16 hedgehogs	3.20
Gerald Ingerson, 1 hedgehog	.20
Clayton Blay, 1 hedgehog	.20
Clinton Harriman, 2 hedgehogs	.40
Wescott Montgomery, 1 hedgehog	.20
Robert Sawyer, 1 hedgehog	.20
Hollis Whitcomb, 1 hedgehog	.20
	$12.40

Detail 9—Damage by Dogs and Fees:

Hollis Whitcomb, fees	$1.60
George Miller, labor	3.60
	$5.20
Detail 10—Dr. H. L. Johnson, health officer	$5.00

Detail 11—Vital Statistics:

Hollis Whitcomb, town clerk	$ 2.00
Bertha Brooks, town clerk	15.00
Charles E. Dixon, registrar	.20
	$17.20

Detail 12—Rubbish and Dump:

John E. Burnham, rubbish signs	$ 4.50
Olcott Aldrich, labor	38.20
Donald Taylor, labor	30.60
Perley Goodwin, labor	9.00

Ernest Herbert, labor	5.40
Garold Miller, labor	9.99
Pliny Goodwin, labor	18.40
	$116.09

Detail 13—Town Maintenance:

Garold Miller, labor	$ 592.11
Donald Taylor, labor	358.00
Ernest Herbert, labor	104.40
Clyde Taylor, labor and truck	40.20
Guy Houghton, labor	20.80
Ernest Nelson, labor	16.60
Warren Miller, labor	13.60
Fred Brooks, labor	13.60
Raymond Miller, labor	4.80
O. N. Aldrich, labor	4.20
Howard Miller, labor	3.20
Rupert Carpenter, labor	2.80
Richard Sullivan, labor	2.60
Arthur Hunt, truck	2.40
Perley Goodwin, labor	.60
	$1,179.91

(Refund to this account of $24.41)

Detail 14—Snow Removal:

Garold Miller, labor	$ 445.23
Donald Taylor, labor	107.40
Quentin Aulis, labor	38.20
Frank Hawes, labor	15.60
Warren Miller, labor	6.80
George Delage, labor	.60
Fred Brooks, labor	1.60
Ernest Herbert, labor	25.60
Clifford Clark, labor	10.80

Howard Miller, labor	3.60
Ernest Nelson, labor	15.60
O. N. Aldrich, labor	14.50
Perley Goodwin, labor	16.40
Paul Welch, labor	1.20
William Carbee, labor	.80
Roscoe Bean, labor	3.20
Edward Hall, labor	22.40
Fred Brooks, rent of shed	5.00
Solvay Sales Corp., chloride	144.00
Vulcan Steel Corp., plow blades	24.43
State Highway Garage, equipment for plow	13.28
Casellini Venable Corp., edges and cable	27.60
State of N. H., plow equipment	2.80
Depot Store, Inc., paper for sand	21.45
Robert Moore, sand	31.35
G. R. Jesseman, express	.65
Peckett's, plowing Bancroft road	2.75

	$1,102.84
Detail 15—Road Oil, State of N. H.	$300.00

Detail 16—Town Road Assistance:

State of N. H., appropriation	$246.76
Solvay Sales Corp., chloride	120.00
	$366.76

(Refund from State of $160.21)

Detail 17—Street Lighting:

Public Service Co. of N. H.	$2,216.25

Detail 18—General Expense Highway Department:

James Wafer, truck expense	$ 226.88
C. M. Vintinner, truck expense	137.65
Central Garage, truck expense	107.26

Elwood Lewis, truck expense	21.43
James Wafer, new truck	475.00
John E. Burnham, road signs	10.50
O. D. Ellingwood, lumber	4.05
C. A. Young, lumber	24.90
Jack Davis, lumber	30.24
O. R. Conrad, lumber	15.51
E. J. McKenzie, bridge planks	74.82
Robert Sherburne, planks	64.96
Mrs. Onyse Fitch, posts for fence	17.00
O. N. Aldrich, labor	14.30
Littleton Hardware Co. Inc., equipment	11.55
F. E. Aldrich & Son, supplies	5.04
R. E. Peabody, Inc., supplies	.80
Depot Store, Inc., grindstone and supplies	28.54
Solvay Sales Corp., chloride	48.00
Wheeling Metal & Mfg. Co., culverts	41.40
N. E. Metal Culvert Co., culverts	11.80
Archie Pelletier, express	1.50
The Peck Company, paint	.75
State Highway Garage, tile	6.70
Casellini Venable Corp., paint and equipment	26.80
State of N. H., patching tar	75.60
Roland Smith, street signs	5.00
Franconia Insurance Agency, compensation, public liability and truck insurance	182.37
Garold Miller, mileage, re. road machine	3.37
	$1,673.72

Detail 19—Libraries:

Dr. H. L. Johnson, appropriation	$200.00
Eva M. A. Cummings, librarian's salary	175.00
	$375.00

Detail 20—Old Age Assistance:

State of N. H.	$293.25

Detail 21—Town Poor:

Case No. 1 (wood purchased $6.21)	$6.44
(refund $12.65)	
Case No. 2 (wood purchased $2.46)	.54
(refund $3.00)	
Lynn L. Bowles	486.11
(credit to this account of $160.00)	
Elizabeth Herbert	4.00
Olcott N. Aldrich	275.85
Lydia Davis	121.50
Mable Carpenter	42.89
Mae Pelletier	4.45
George Miller	257.00
(Cancer Commission paid $8.25)	
(Refund of $5.00 by Warren Miller)	
Transients (refund 5c)	15.25
	$1,214.03

Detail 22—County Poor:

County soldier	$ 30.00
Stella Little	123.50
Guy L. Harriman	211.41
Alvin L. Wood	4.00
Wescott Montgomery	2.75
	$371.66

(Grafton County refunded $367.66)

Detail 23—Soldier's Aid: $116.54
(This account secured by mortgage given Town)

Detail 24—Memorial Day:
Senior class, for wreaths $25.00

Detail 25—Advertising:
Ray Plummer, recreational guide $ 92.22

Franconia Notch Area Association	300.00
White Mountain Region	101.00
John E. Burnham, directory sign	130.00
Martha E. Carpenter, solicit adv. for sign	6.00
Ellingwood Trucking Co., deliver sign	6.00
Lyle Signs, small town sign	33.44
Archie Pelletier, express sign	.35
Courier Printing Co., advertising folders	165.50
	$834.51

(Credit of $119.72 to this account)

Detail 26—Parks and Playgrounds:

Garold Miller, labor	$ 14.04
George Delage, labor	.80
William Carbee, labor	2.60
O. N. Aldrich, labor	14.40
Donald Taylor, labor	8.80
Wayside Gardens, flowers	6.25
	$46.89

Detail 27—Special Summer Traffic Patrol:

Merton Shores, labor	$115.00

Detail 28—Cemeteries:

Willow cemetery: $260.62

Fred Brooks, labor	$99.00
Pliny Goodwin, labor	86.40
The Peck Co., paint	62.01
G. R. Jesseman, express on paint	1.91
Depot Store, brushes	2.60
Fred Brooks, raw oil	3.60
E. J. McKenzie, lumber	5.10

Elmwood cemetery: $402.36

Garold Miller, labor on roads	$10.26
Donald Taylor, labor	6.00
Perley Goodwin, labor	1.20

Fred F. Brooks, labor	33.80
Albert J. Delage, man and horses	4.80
Pearl H. Bowles, Sexton	294.40
Water rent	12.00
Edward Hall, labor	.40
George H. Stevens, resetting stones	28.00
Pearl H. Bowles, repairs to mower	2.00
Montgomery Ward Co., wheelbarrow	6.45
G. Robert Jesseman, freight on wheelbarrow	1.10
Roland E. Peabody, Inc., supplies	1.95
	$662.98

Deetail 29—Legal Expense:

F. J. Shores, registrar	$19.76
Henry A. Dodge, Attorney	31.15
	$50.91

Detail 30—Taxes Bought by the Town:

Nat'l. F. Perkins Estate, April sale	$1,230.41
Elizabeth Later Estate, April sale	46.11
Ruth Carpenter	16.00
Frank Hawes	32.00
Guy Harriman	23.11
Ernest Herbert	62.22
Charles Kosch	31.81
Warren Miller	23.11
J. P. Collins & H. P. Cross	67.31
George Dexter	5.11
Forest Products Co.	17.53
Mrs. E. Huntington	38.86
Nat'l. Perkins Estate	999.64
Elizabeth Later Estate	45.97
	$2,639.19

Detail 31—State of N. H.:
.Moving shovel $66.20

Detail 32—F. H. Jesseman, refund of 1938
    overpayment $37.00

Detail 33—Norman Fox, Lisbon Town Clerk:
  Refund of licenses   . $26.31

Detail 34—Land Damages:
  John B. Eames $1.00
  Laura S. Corey   1.00
  Eugene Cray   1.00
  Roscoe Bean   1.00
                                            _____
                                            $4.00

Detail 35—Refund of taxes:
  Hazel Bean $26.53

Detail 36—Bertha Brooks, overpayment $14.71

Detail 37—Interest:
  Littleton Savings bank, temporary loans $ 6.67
  Littleton National bank, temporary loans   18.45
  F. W. Horne Co., temporary loans   110.00
  Littleton Nat'l bank, bonds and notes   1,755.00
  Lisbon Sav. Bank & Trust Co., note   40.00
                                          _____
                                  $1,930.12
(Refund of $110.00 from F. W. Horne Co.)

Detail 38—Sidewalk Construction and Repair:
  Construction account: $206.29
    William Carbee, labor $32.00
    Raymond Miller, labor   17.40
    Alison Berwick, labor   19.80

Walter Eaton, labor	18.60
Morrill Locke, mixer	8.40
Depot Store, Inc., cement	84.70
Central Garage, gas for mixer	.39
Carl Nelson, forms	25.00

Regular sidewalk account: $127.94

Clyde Taylor, plow and sand	$59.35
A. E. Morse, railing	18.97
Warren Miller, labor	14.40
Garold Miller, labor	9.72
Donald Taylor, labor	7.20
Walter J. Pelletier, boards	1.50
O. N. Aldrich, labor	2.80
Harry Nelson, labor	3.60
Archie Taylor, labor	1.20
Fred Brooks, plowing	5.00
George Delage, sand	1.20
William Heath, labor	3.00
	$334.23

Detail 39—New Equipment:

Casellini Venable Corp., grader	$384.24
G. R. Jesseman, freight on grader	26.55
Archie Pelletier, freight on grader	3.74
	$414.53

Detail 40—Indebtedness Payments:

Littleton Savings bank, temporary loans	$ 2,000.00
Littleton Nat'l. bank, temporary loans	17,000.00
Lisbon Sav. Bank & Trust Co., pumper notes	1,000.00
Littleton Nat'l. bank, payment on bonds	2,500.00
Littleton Nat'l. bank, water works note	1,000.00
	$23,500.00

Detail 41—Grafton Co. Treas., for tax $4,375.34

Detail 42—School Payments:
- R. E. Peabody, treasurer, bal. 1938 account $6,751.20
- R. E. Peabody, treasurer, a/c 1939 appro.   6,000.00

     $12,751.20

Water Department Report

RECEIPTS

January 1, 1939, cash on hand	$ 947.21	
Water rentals	1,421.70	
Sale of equipment	32.50	
Patrons—piping service lines	27.35	$2,428.76

PAYMENTS

Town of Franconia, note, 1938	$1,000.00	
A. E. Morse, labor	217.55	
Henry A. Dodge, legal expenses	271.49	
W. I. Richardson, surveying	5.00	
Postage	2.50	
R. E. Peabody, Inc., supplies	.90	
Hollis H. Whitcomb, commissioner	17.50	
Harry P. Carpenter, commissioner	62.50	
Frank Sanborn, commissioner	14.00	
Dr. H. L. Johnson, commissioner	50.00	
Victor L. Clark, commissioner	40.00	
Total payments	$1,681.44	
January 1, 1940, cash on hand	747.32	$2,428.76

ASSETS

Cash on hand	$747.32	
Water rentals due (arrears)	75.50	$822.82

Excess of Liabilities over Assets $177.18

     $1,000.00

LIABILITIES

Town of Franconia, 1939 note $1,000.00

STATEMENT OF INDEBTEDNESS

Due Town of Franconia, note issue	$11,000.00
Due Town of Franconia, bond issue	25,000.00
January 1, 1940, current debt	177.18

Total net debt $36,177.18

Abbie Greenleaf Library

RECEIPTS

Cash on hand, February 1, 1939	$984.89	
Received from Greenleaf Trust	479.30	
Received from appropriation	200.00	
Received from interest	15.65	$1,679.84

PAYMENTS

A. E. Berwick	$ 68.10
Public Service Co. of N. H.	19.16
Littleton Hardware Co., Inc.	2.75
Depot Store, Inc.	2.15
Clyde Taylor	4.00
H. R. Huntting Co.	124.36
B. Roberts	3.00
A. E. Morse	5.43
Gaylord Brothers	4.55
American Library Asso.	3.00
Metropolitan Church Asso.	3.50
Eva Cummings	25.00
Goodspeeds Bookshop	3.15
Junior Literary Guild	40.10
Crowley & Lunt	10.00
Franconia Water Dept.	2.50
Gowing & Chamberlain	500.00
J. J. Coney	.50
Colonial Beacon Oil Co.	43.50
W. B. Fosgate	5.80
Harlan Little	30.00
To balance with bank	.10
	$900.65

Cash on hand February 1, 1940   349.08
Cash in Savings Bank   430.11 $1,679.84

LIBRARIAN'S REPORT

RECEIPTS

Balance at beginning of year	$11.25
Fines	10.05
Other sources	3.46
	$24.76
Total expenditures	22.64
Balance on hand	$2.12
Number bound volumes Jan. 31, 1939	7,490
Added by purchase	156
Added by gift	40
	7,686
Withdrawn	17
Total on hand, January 31, 1940	7,669

SERVICE

	Adults	Juvenile	Total
Number vol. non-fiction loaned	1,057	325	1,382
Number volumes fiction loaned	4,169	1,606	5,775
Unbound magazines loaned			700
			7,857
Number of new borrowers for year			23
Total number active borrowers			203

48

Number magazines received   26
Respectfully submitted,
EVA M. Ä. CUMMINGS,
Librarian

AUDITOR'S STATEMENT

This is to certify that I have examined the accounts of the Selectmen, Treasurer, Tax Collector, Town Clerk, Water Commissioners, Library Trustees, and Trustees of Trust Funds and find them to be correct to the best of my knowledge and belief.

LOUISE H. VINTINNER

February 16, 1940   Auditor

Willow Cemetery
Income

Balance in check book January 1st, 1939	$ 31.55
Interest to June	3.75
Total Income Willow Cemetery	$ 35.30

Expenditures

19 hours labor, cleaning and straightening stones	$ 7.60
Materials used in cleaning stones	.62
Mowing, loam and seed	5.00
Total Expenditures in Willow Cemetery	$ 13.22
*Cash on hand in check book, Willow Cemetery (J. B. Rideout lot)	$ 22.08

Elmwood Cemetery
Income

Balance in check book January 1st, 1939	$107.30
Interest to June	131.19
Total Income Elmwood Cemetery	$238.49

Expenditures

Driver of town truck (loam given by Mr. Bodwell)	$ 4.70
330 hours labor	132.00
W. B. Phillips, flowers	5.00
20 pounds grass seed	6.22
Monument cleaner	10.58
Brushes	1.20

5½ squares shingles	24.75
Ridge boards	1.00
22 pounds nails	1.54
½ ton lawn phosphate	26.50
Supervising work and treasurer, 1939	25.00

Total Expenditures Elmwood Cemetery	$238.49
*Balance in check book, Littleton National Bank, November 29th, 1939	$ 22.08

February 1, 1940
REPORT OF TRUST FUNDS
Town of Franconia, New Hampshire

Income

Interest received on Trust Funds	$278.54
Contribution from Miss Helen M. Oakes for care of graves	3.00
	$281.54

Expenditures

January 1, 1939, interest on all Trust Funds in the Littleton Savings Bank (46)	$134.94

(This total amount, $134.94, deposited in June, 1939, in The Littleton National Bank to the credit of Town of Franconia, Trustee Funds, Myra Sherburn, Treasurer.)

Amount of Income in Littleton Savings Bank	$274.14

This amount represents July 1, 1939, and January 1, 1940, interest on all Trust Funds (48) except two deposited in the Lisbon Savings Bank & Trust Co., Savings Department.

Amount of Income in Lisbon Savings Bank and Trust Company, Savings Department	$9.20
Total Income on Hand in Trust Funds February 1, 1940	$283.34
Contribution, Miss Helen M. Oakes, in safe-deposit with Trust Fund bank books	3.00
Total Income on Hand, February 1, 1940	$286.34

Report of the Trust Funds of the Town of Franconia on February 1, 1940

Date of Creation	TRUST FUNDS — PURPOSE OF CREATION (All trust funds should be reported giving name of fund and donor.)	HOW INVESTED	Amount of Principal	Balance of Income on Hand at Beginning of Year	Income During Year	Expended During Year	Balance of Income on Hand at End of Year
1931	...r McKenzie	In Savings Bank & Trust Co.	$ 91.21	$ 2.29	$ 2.10		4.39
1933	George Kerr	In Savings Bank & Trust Co.	100.00	2.51	2.30		4.81
1901	J. B. ...	In Savings Bank	300.00	3.75	7.54	3.75	7.54
1920	H. W. ...	In Savings Bank	200.00	2.50	5.03	2.50	5.03
1920	M. A. ...	In Savings Bank	100.00	1.25	2.51	1.25	2.51
1920	...	In Savings Bank	100.00	1.25	2.51	1.25	2.51
1920	...y Spooner	In Savings Bank	50.00	.63	1.26	.63	1.26
1920	S. C. ...	In Savings Bank	50.00	.63	1.26	.63	1.26
1920	W. B. ...	In Savings Bank	28.00	.35	.70	.35	.70
1920	...	In Savings Bank	300.00	3.75	7.54	3.75	7.54
1920	...y W. ...	In Savings Bank	100.00	1.25	2.51	1.25	2.51
1922	Byron Richardson	In Savings Bank	100.00	1.25	2.51	1.25	2.51
1923	Ivory N. ...	In Savings Bank	100	1.25	2.51	1.25	2.51
1923	...e N. M. Bean	In Savings Bank	100.00	1.25	2.51	1.25	2.51
1924	Kilburn D. Priest	In Savings Bank	200.00	2.50	5.03	2.50	5.03
1925	Ella H. Bishop	In Savings Bank	75.00	.94	1.88	.94	1.88
1925	... Knight	In Savings Bank	200.00	2.50	5.03	2.50	5.03
1926	Edward H. Wells	In Savings Bank	100.00	1.25	2.51	1.25	2.51
1926	...s M. Smith	In Savings Bank	100.00	1.25	2.51	1.25	2.51
1926	...s Wills &	In Savings Bank	100.00	1.25	2.51	1.25	2.51
1926	E. H. ...	In Savings Bank	200.00	2.50	5.03	2.50	5.03
1926	Frank H. ...	In Savings Bank	100.00	1.25	2.51	1.25	2.51
1926	...t H. Spooner	Littleton Savings Bank	50.00	.63	1.26	.63	1.26

Year	Name	Bank	Principal				
1926	Otis Brooks	Littleton Savings Bank	50.00	.63	1.26	.63	1.26
1926	Milo J. Corliss	Littleton Savings Bank	100.00	1.25	2.51	1.25	2.51
1926	George Glines	Littleton Savings Bank	50.00	.63	1.26	.63	1.26
1926	Wilbur F. Parker	Littleton Savings Bank	200.00	2.50	5.03	2.50	5.03
1927	Emma J. Cheney	Littleton Savings Bank	100.00	1.25	2.51	1.25	2.51
1928	Alba A. Glover	Littleton Savings Bank	50.00	.63	1.26	.63	1.26
1929	W. B. Chase	Littleton Savings Bank	100.00	1.25	2.51	1.25	2.51
1929	Josephine S. Harris	Littleton Savings Bank	100.00	1.25	2.51	1.25	2.51
1930	B. D. and R. S. Callendar	Littleton Savings Bank	100.00	1.25	2.51	1.25	2.51
1930	George H. Kendall	Littleton Savings Bank	100.00	1.25	2.51	1.25	2.51
1930	Edward B. Parker	Littleton Savings Bank	100.00	1.25	2.51	1.25	2.51
1932	Edward D. and Lizzie B. Chase	Littleton Savings Bank	100.00	1.25	2.51	1.25	2.51
1934	Roswell Knights	Littleton Savings Bank	100.00	1.25	2.51	1.25	2.51
1934	Fred L. Harris	Littleton Savings Bank	100.00	1.25	2.51	1.25	2.51
1934	Maude M. Bishop	Littleton Savings Bank	100.00	1.25	2.51	1.25	2.51
1936	Noah Wells	Littleton Savings Bank	100.00	1.25	2.51	1.25	2.51
1936	Charles Fred Edson	Littleton Savings Bank	100.00	1.25	2.51	1.25	2.51
1937	Frank H. and Fred G. Sanborn	Littleton Savings Bank	100.00	1.25	2.51	1.25	2.51
1937	Elmore Whipple	Littleton Savings Bank	100.00	1.25	2.51	1.25	2.51
1937	George Young, Charles B., and Willis J. Young	Littleton Savings Bank	225.00	2.81	5.65	2.81	5.65
1937	Lucy A. Priest	Littleton Savings Bank	300.00	3.75	7.54	3.75	7.54
1937	Willis B. Phillips	Littleton Savings Bank	5,614.32	70.18	141.23	70.18	141.23
1938	Manson R. York	Littleton Savings Bank	50.00	.63	1.26	.63	1.26
1938	Mindwell A. Cadarette	Littleton Savings Bank	50.00	.63	1.26	.63	1.26
1938	Luder M. Clark	Littleton Savings Bank	100.00	.62	2.51	.62	2.51
1939	Faust M. Weisman	Littleton Savings Bank	50.00		1.15		1.15
1939	Lizzie M. Kendall	Littleton Savings Bank	100.00		.42		.42
			$11,183.53	$139.74	$278.54	$134.94	$283.34

NOTE: Rate of Interest 2.5% except for first two items on which the rate is 2.25%.

This is to certify that the information contained in this report is complete and correct, to the best of our knowledge and belief.

Franconia School District
Report for 1939-1940

DISTRICT OFFICERS
School Board

Dr. H. L. Johnson, chairman	Term expires 1942
Mrs. Charlotte Sawyer	Term expires 1941
Clare T. Bodwell	Term expires 1940

Superintendent of Schools
F. Lester Trafton

Other District Officers

Mrs. Martha Herbert	Moderator
Paul Rich	Clerk
Roland E. Peabody	Treasurer
Mrs. Martha Carpenter	Auditor
Fred H. Jesseman	

Truant Officer and Census Enumerator

TEACHERS, DOW ACADEMY

Gilbert Rhoades, Headmaster	French and Latin
Jere Chase, Submaster	Science and Mathematics
Louise Nute	English and History
Claire Paddleford	Home Economics
Kathleen Callahan	Grades 5 and 6
Florence Blanchard	Grades 3 and 4
Alice Bewley	Grades 1 and 2

School Meeting Warrant

Town Hall, March 12, 1940, 2:00 P. M.
ARTICLES TO BE ACTED UPON

1. To choose a Moderator for the coming year.

2. To choose a Clerk for the ensuing year.

3. To choose a Member of the School Board for the coming three years.

4. To choose a Treasurer for the ensuing year.

5. To determine and appoint the salaries of the School Board and Truant Officer, and fix the compensation of any other officers or agents of the district.

6. To hear the reports of agents, auditors, committees, or officers heretofore chosen, and pass any vote relating thereto.

7. To choose agents, auditors, and committees in relation to any subject embraced in this warrant.

8. To see if the District will vote to make an alteration in the amount of money required to be assessed for the ensuing year for the support of public schools and the payment of statutory obligations of the District, as determined by the School Board in its annual report.

9. To elect a trustee to serve on the Board of Trustees of Dow Academy.

10. To transact any other business that may legally come before the meeting.

H. L. JOHNSON,
CLARE T. BODWELL,
CHARLOTTE SAWYER,
School Board.

Financial Report—District of Franconia

	Paid out 1938-1939	Budget 1939-1940	Paid out to Feb. 14	Budget 1940-1941
ADMINISTRATION				
1. Salaries of district officers	$ 105.00	$ 105.00	$ 110.00	$ 110.00
2. Superintendent's excess salary	254.54	254.54	254.54	254.54
3. Truant officer and census	10.00	10.00	10.00	10.00
4. Expenses of administration	185.70	150.00	90.76	150.00
INSTRUCTION				
5. Teachers' salaries	9,125.00	9,600.00	5,730.00	9,900.00
6. Textbooks	229.85	225.00	236.70	225.00
7. Scholars' supplies	387.35	350.00	281.68	350.00
8. Flags, etc.	1.35	10.00		10.00
9. Other expenses of instruction	184.59	110.00	71.23	110.00
OPERATION AND MAINTENANCE				
10. Janitor service	738.00	738.00	414.00	738.00
11. Fuel	57.50	600.00	242.50	600.00
12. Water, light, janitor's supplies	293.41	350.00	230.93	350.00
13. Minor repairs and expenses	360.23	350.00	477.24	350.00
AUXILIARY AGENCIES				
14. Medical inspection	290.00	290.00	240.00	290.00
15. Transportation of pupils	1,083.75	1,090.00	553.25	1,090.00
18. Other special activities	47.65	150.00	22.10	150.00
FIXED CHARGES				
19. Per capita tax	242.00	262.00	262.00	224.00
20. Insurance and other fixed charges	40.00	60.00	12.50	
CONSTRUCTION AND EQUIPMENT				
22. Alterations of old buildings	12.05		230.00	
23. New equipment	45.36	250.00	534.41	250.00
DEBT, INTEREST. AND OTHER. CHARGES				
26. Payments of notes or bills from previous year	625.18		395.21	
Total payments for all purposes	$14,318.51	$14,954.54	$10,399.05	$15,161.54

Summary of Receipts and Payments

July 1, 1938, to June 30, 1939
RECEIPTS

Appropriation	$12,725.00
Tuitions	2,325.12
Receipts from trust funds	374.29
Sale of supplies, rent, etc.	150.28
Dog taxes, 1938	26.20
Cash on hand, July 1, 1938	1,015.96

Total Receipts $16,616.85

PAYMENTS

Orders from the School Board	$14,318.51
Cash on hand, June 30, 1939	2,298.34

Total $16,616.85

AUDITOR'S CERTIFICATE

This is to certify that I have examined the books and other financial records of the School Board of Franconia, of which this is a true summary for the fiscal year ending June 30, 1939, and find them correctly cast and properly vouched.

MARTHA CARPENTER,

July 15, 1939   Auditor

REPORT OF DISTRICT TREASURER
Fiscal Year Ending June 30, 1939

Cash on hand June 30, 1938		$ 1,015.96
Received from Selectmen:		
Appropriations	$12,725.00	
Dog taxes	26.20	

Income from trust funds — 374.29
Received from tuitions — 2,325.12
Received from all other sources — 150.28

$15,600.89

Total Amount (balance and receipts) — $16,616.85
Less School Board orders paid — 14,318.51

Balance on hand as of June 30, 1939 — $2,298.34
(Treasurer's bank balance)

ROLAND E. PEABODY,
July 6, 1939 — Treasurer.

ESTIMATED RECEIPTS
1939-1940

Cash on hand, July 1, 1939 — $ 2,298.34
Appropriation — 11,600.00
Tuitions — 2,100.00
Dog taxes, 1939 — 90.00
Income from trust funds — 375.00

Total Estimated Receipts — $16,555.00
Less total estimated expenditures,
(July 1, 1939, to June 30, 1940) — 16,500.00

Estimated Balance, June 30, 1940 — 55.00

School Board's Estimate for 1940-1941

School Board's statement of amount required to support public schools and meet other statutory obligations of the District for the fiscal year beginning July 1, 1940,

DETAILED STATEMENT OF EXPENDITURES

Support of Schools:

Teachers' salaries	$ 9,900.00
Textbooks	225.00
Scholars' supplies	350.00
Flags, etc.	10.00
Other expenses of instruction	110.00
Janitor service	738.00
Fuel	600.00
Water, light, janitor's supplies	350.00
Minor repairs and expenses	350.00
Health supervision	290.00
Transportation of pupils	1,090.00
Other special activities	150.00

$14,163.00

Other Statutory Requirements:

Salaries of district officers (fixed by district)	$110.00
Truant officer and school census (fixed by district)	10.00
Superintendent's excess salary (fixed by supervisory union)	254.54
Per capita tax (reported by State Treasurer)	224.00
Other obligations	400.00

$998.54

Total amount required to meet school
board's budget $15,161.54

ESTIMATED INCOME OF DISTRICT

Dog taxes	$ 90.00
Income from trust funds	375.00

High and elementary school
.tuitions   -   1,900.00

Deduct total estimated income‑
   (not raised by taxation) $2,365.00

Balance to be assessed $12,796.54

We recommend that the District raise and appropriate the sum of $12,800.00 for the next school year.

Respectfully submitted,

H. L. JOHNSON,

C. T. BODWELL,

CHARLOTTE SAWYER,

School Board.

Itemized Expenditures

1938-1939

ADMINISTRATION

1. **Salaries of District Officers:**

Martha Carpenter, auditing	$ 5.00
Roland E. Peabody	25.00
Dr. H. L. Johnson	25.00
C. T. Bodwell	25.00
Charlotte Sawyer	25.00 ˘

                                             $105.00

2. **Superintendent's Excess Salary:**
Grace W. Hoskins, union treasurer   254.54

3. **Truant Officer and School Census:**
Fred H. Jesseman   10.00

4. **Expenses of Administration:**

Willis Herbert, envelopes	$ 5.01
Grace W. Hoskins, treasurer, union expenses	47.74
N. E. Telephone & Telegraph Co., telephone charges	54.01

Gilbert Rhoades, miscellaneous expense 11.88
Courier Printing Co., letter-
heads, envelopes and vouch-
ers 17.44
Lisbon Job Printing, report
cards 4.75
Commercial Press Inc. 3.75
Edson C. Eastman, account
book 3.00
G. H. Rice and Co., record
book and cards 18.72
Dr. H. L. Johnson, telephone 2.30
F. Lester Trafton, trips for
teachers 13.00
Lisbon Special School District, miscellaneous expenses 4.10

$185.70

INSTRUCTION

5. Teachers' Salaries:

Gilbert Rhoades	$2,000.00
Jeremiah Chase	1,700.00
Louise Nute	1,000.00
Barbara Vogel	1,000.00
Kathleen Callahan	1,096.00
Alice Bewley	1,025.00
Kermit Bennett	400.00
La Myra Harriman	838.00
Mrs. Elizabeth Moore, sub- stitute	16.00
Madeline Whitcomb, substi- tute	40.00
Martha Carpenter, substitute	10.00

$9,125.00

6. Textbooks:

John C. Winston Company	$21.88
Harcourt and Brace	41.25
Charles Scribner's Sons	18.60
Row Peterson Company	7.78
University of Nebraska	7.00
Allyn and Bacon	8.05
Arlo Publishing Company	6.81
Ginn and Company	3.77
Macmillan Company	15.24
American Book Company	32.50
Scott Foresman	28.94
Edward E. Babb Company	2.08
Noble and Noble	2.56
D. C. Heath and Company	3.25
Bobbs-Merrill Company	9.77
Silver Burdett Company	9.45
L. W. Singer	7.72
Lisbon Special School District	3.20
	$229.85

7. Scholars' Supplies:

National Geographic Society	$ 3.50
Reader's Digest Association	5.00
Gilbert Rhoades, expense	.50
Archie J. Pelletier, freight	6.00
J. L. Hammett Company	98.37
American Education Press	20.00
Cambosco Scientific Company	1.15
Carl Larson, supplies	21.58
Phillips' Ribbon and Carbon Co.	7.50
Goudie's Hardware Store, supplies	10.17

Thompson Manufacturing Co., manual training supplies	7.96
Webster Publishing Company	5.73
Lyons and Carnahan, spelling books	7.70
Scott Foresman, work books	11.15
Phillips Paper Company	1.38
Robert Sawyer, magazine subscription	2.50
Roland E. Peabody, supplies	5.13
Edward E. Babb Company, supplies	60.97
Welles Publishing Company, reference books	3.00
H. A. Eaton and Son, manual training supplies	16.00
Civic Educational Service	5.00
F. E. Aldrich & Son, supplies	26.49
Macmillan Company	1.26
Union Leader Publishing Co., subscription to paper	3.00
University of Nebraska	7.00
The Depot Store, supplies	2.24
Allyn and Bacon, work books	2.92
MacLeod's Inc., supplies	1.85
H. A. Moore, manual training supplies	21.35
Carl Larson, pencils	10.31
Littleton Hardware Co., supplies	3.65
Lisbon Special School District, supplies	6.99

$387.35

8. Flags and Appurtenances:
Lisbon Special School District, supplies (flag) $1.35

9. Other Expenses of Instruction:

Gilbert Rhoades, orchestra and teachers' reception	$14.00
Edward McKenzie, sawdust	3.00
The Depot Store	1.40
Ginn and Company, reference books	2.80
The Quarrie Company, encyclopedias	78.70
Bobbs-Merrill Company, reference books	2.67
D. C. Heath Company, reference books	2.38
Scott Foresman & Co., reference books	9.46
American Book Company, reference book	1.71
World Book Company, tests	12.93
McGraw-Hill Company, reference books	1.37
Houghton-Mifflin, reference book	1.72
Macmillan Company, reference books	2.82
Cleveland Safety Council, reference books	2.69
Lyons-Carnahan, reference books	2.56
Silver Burdett Company, reference books	4.50
Thomas Nelson, reference books	1.05
J. L. Hammett, diplomas and covers	15.33
Treasurer, senior class, reception expense	15.00

M. H. Watson, engrossing
diplomas   2.75
Lisbon Special School District, supplies   5.75

$184.59

OPERATION AND MAINTENANCE

10. Janitor Service:
E. M. Blodgett $594.00
Merton Shores   144.00

$738.00

11. Fuel:
Edward McKenzie, slabwood $25.00
George Miller, sawing wood   2.50
Percy Leighton, fuel   30.00

$57.50

12. Water, Light and Janitor Supplies:
Public Service Company, elec-
tricity $187.46
Roland E. Peabody, supplies   4.34
West Disinfecting Company,
supplies   11.55
Masury Young Company, sup-
plies   56.64
Franconia Water Company,
water rent   18.00
F. E. Aldrich   4.47
Cheshire Chemical Co., dust-void   3.50
Depot Store, supplies   7.45

$293.41

13. Minor Repairs and Expense:
Pauline Austen, cleaning
school building $60.00

E. M. Blodgett, cleaning floors   18.50

Harry Siegel, tuning piano   5.00

A. W. Farr and Company,
  window glass   2.00

West Disinfecting Company,
  supplies   41.75

Gilbert Rhoades, repairs   1.60

Gowing and Chamberlin,
  repairs on radiator   8.40

Littleton Hardware Co., air-
  valves   20.43

Treasurer, U. S., stage set   90.00

Roland E. Peabody, glass
  and putty   2.85

J. H. Fadden & Son, shingles   90.63

E. R. Forbush, clocks repaired   1.75

Paul Trippett, Fyr-Fyter
  refills   9.00

Herbert Bassett, painting
  flag pole   5.00

Elwood W. Lewis, repairs
  on swings   1.50

The Depot Store, supplies   1.82

$360.23

SPECIAL ACTIVITIES

14. **Medical Inspection:**

Littleton Community Nurs-
  ing Association, salary,
  Miss Bryant $200.00

Miss Marion Cass, treasurer, transportation of Miss
  Bryant   50.00

Dr. H. L. Johnson, medical
inspection   40.00

                                          $290.00

15. **Transportation:**
Archie Pelletier $570.00
Howard E. Miller   50.75
Jack Barrett   83.00
Perry Ball   380.00

           $1,083.75

18. **Other Special Activities:**
Roland E. Peabody $ 2.70
Littleton Hardware Company 1.95
Walter H. Baker Company,
playbooks   3.00
Archie Pelletier, transpor-
tation to four carnivals 40.00

           $47.65

FIXED CHARGES
19. **Insurance:**
Franconia Insurance Com-
pany, insurance $40.00

20. **Other Fixed Charges:**
State treasurer, per capita tax $242.00

CONSTRUCTION AND EQUIPMENT
22. **Alterations of Old Buildings:**
Victor Clark, plumbing in
old P. O. building $12.05

23. **New Equipment:**
Cambosco Scientific Com-
pany, equipment $36.45
Montgomery Ward Company,
band-saw blade   .91

West Disinfecting Company,
soap dispenser   2.00
Littleton Hardware Company,
supplies   6.00

             $45.36

DEBT SERVICE

26. Old Bills:

Roland Peabody, miscellaneous expense $ 1.59
Roland Currier, miscellaneous expense   6.09
H. L. Heald, petition special
meeting   10.00
M. H. Watson, transporta-
tion to Laconia   12.50
Town of Franconia, 85 cords
wood at 7.00   595.00

             $625.18

Total Expenditures 1938-1939 $14,318.51

Report of the Superintendent of Schools

To the School Board and Citizens of Franconia:

The enrollment of your schools last year was 160, the average membership 141.61 and the percent of attendance 93.73. Epidemics of illness were responsible for a lower percent of attendance than for the previous year. There were 19 tuition pupils in the academy and 26 in the elementary school.

This year the total enrollment to date is 156. The present enrollment by grades is as follows: grades one and two, 26; grades three and four, 23; grades five and six, 21; grades seven and eight 30; and grades nine to twelve 50. There are 24 tuition pupils in the academy and 15 in the elementary school.

There were only two changes in the teaching staff this year. Miss Claire Paddleford succeeded Miss Vogel as teacher of home economics and junior high subjects. Miss Paddleford is a graduate of Keene Teachers' College. Miss Florence Blanchard returned to teach grades three and four again.

During the past year a new set of scenery and a new velour curtain have been made for the stage in the assembly hall by Mr. William Newton. These add much, both to the appearance and use of the stage. The project was financed jointly by the federal government, the School Board, and the teachers.

A new series of arithmetic texts was introduced this year. These books are an improvement over the ones previously used, and should increase the efficiency of the teaching in this important subject. New literature books were bought for the junior-senior English class.

Although the fire caused the loss of the home economics equipment it has resulted in an improved gymnasium and two rooms much better adapted for both home economics and manual training. The home economics room has been re-equipped with a new electric range, new tables, cupboards, etc. It is a room of which the school is justly proud. Mr. Bodwell has been of great assistance in the purchase of equipment.

It is planned to move the manual training equipment into the lower room of the gymnasium building next fall. There is still a large room on the second floor which should be finished off into two locker rooms in the near future.

The Greenleaf Civics Club is again providing a hot dish for noon lunch during the winter months.

I wish to thank the members of the School Board and the teachers for their cooperation.

Respectfully submitted,
F. LESTER TRAFTON,
Superintendent of Schools.

Statistical Table of the Franconia Schools
1938-1939

	Total Enrollment	Average Membership	Percent of Attendance	Tardiness
Dow Academy	49	42.861	93.649	55
Grades 7 and 8	34	28.230	94.676	11
Grades 5 and 6	29	27.604	93.794	4
Grades 3 and 4	26	24.034	92.673	29
Grades 1 and 2	19	18.885	94.281	13

Roll of Perfect Attendance

Grades 9-12: Helen Hunt, William Dowell.

Grades 7-8: Rachel Ball, Aner Murray, Bertha Taylor.

Grades 5-6: Ruby Aldrich, Marjorie Herbert, Myrtle Taylor, George Dowell.

Grades 3-4: Rudolph Nelson.

The Report of the School Nurse

Physical examinations of October, 1939 showed the following defects in 145 pupils:

Dental	57
Tonsil conditions	6
Vision	16
Heart condition	3
Anaemia	5
Underweights (10%)	34

Corrections made during 1938-39:

Tonsil operations	7

Vision corrections	16
Dental corrections	22

Dental clinics are held twice a month and vision clinics are held once a month. A tonsil clinic was held in July and contact cases were examined at a tuberculosis clinic.

HAZEL H. BRYANT,

January 30, 1940·   School-Nurse.

Lightning Source UK Ltd.
Milton Keynes UK
UKHW052035191218
334046UK00008BA/762/P